IMPORTANT CONTACT INFORMATION

The following contact information provides important resources for pre-trip planning and situational updates on your location during your trip.

Smart Traveler Enrollment Program

Registration with the US embassy for contact in the event of an emergency and for situational updates on local safety and security.

https://step.state.gov/

Overseas Advisory Security Council

A joint venture between the US State Department and private industry that provides country and city-related safety and security reports.

https://www.osac.gov/

Country Advisory Map

A US State Department updated map of the world showing US Embassy and Consular representation and country security alerts.

https://travelmaps.state.gov/TSGMap/

US Centers for Disease Control

Country-specific guidance on health threats, health tips, and pre-travel vaccine and medicine information.

https://wwwnc.cdc.gov/travel/destinations/list/

Travel Responsibly, Informed & Protected

A resource created by the US Travel Insurance Association providing articles on travel safety, security and health concerns.

http://trip.ustia.org/

CONTINGENCY PLANNING

PRE-TRIP PLANNING

Before you leave on your trip, create a security checklist for your family and work associates:

- Instruct family/work not to provide details about your travel plans to unknown persons

- Leave your contact information – hotel name, number, address, foreign office name, foreign office number, foreign office address

- Schedule times to contact your family and office

- Leave an emergency contact for family and friends to use, should you not call within 24 hours of pre-arranged time

Before you leave on your trip, create your own 'Action List' to take with you:

- U.S. embassy/consulate address and contact number in the country of your travel

- Address and contact number of alternate friendly embassy/consulate, e.g. UK, Australia, Canada

- Map of city showing main roads and arteries

- Mark addresses of police stations, fire stations, hospitals and other safe havens on map

- Mark subway/rail, hotels across city that can be used as a safe house on the map

- Locate a rally point where you can meet other agency personnel in the event of interrupted communications

Plan for emergency transportation use a private service:

- List the contact telephone numbers for travelers who are accompanying you

PRE-TRIP PLANNING (continued)

- Plan to pack food/snacks in the event travel arrangements are delayed or medical reasons require food intake
- Make a list of safety equipment which will be necessary to visit the contractor facility to ensure safety from exposure to dangerous or radioactive materials, and send the equipment in advance of the trip
- Plan to have necessary medications re-filled prior to the trip so your supply will be adequate for your trip
- Determine if your hotel offers private car service prior to your departure
- Identify alternative recognized hotels that offer car services in the event that your hotel service is unavailable when needed
- As a further contingency, identify a second alternative private car service (can be another hotel or recommended private service)
- Do not book a private car in advance - only book when required

CITY/COUNTRY EGRESS PLANNING

Think about how you will safely get out of the city or country in an emergency.

Plan alternate access and routes to the airport.

Plan for emergency transportation via private car service:

Plan an alternate egress from the city/country if the airport is inaccessible:

- Modes of transportation – bus, car, rail, bicycle
- Road route
- Safe house, sanctuary, or force protection, e.g. police station
- Plan how to communicate with embassy/consulate, local police, family and work before and during your egress
- Do not hitchhike

FOREIGN CUSTOMS AND IMMIGRATION

Many countries require entry visas. Prior to travel, you must ensure that you have the appropriate entry visa and meet all requirements. The U.S. State Department, Bureau of Consular Affairs website provides country-specific information including entry, exit and visa requirements. Check the website before leaving, to ensure you meet all requirements.

Many countries also place restrictions on what is allowed into and out of their countries. These restrictions can include:

- Food
- Medications
- Currency
- Electronic Equipment
- Religious possessions or literature

Before traveling, check your destination's customs rules using the same country information on the U.S. State Department, Bureau of Consular Affairs website. If the information you are seeking is not listed, contact the embassy or consulate of the foreign country in the U.S. A simple Internet search for the foreign country embassy in the U.S. will provide contact information.

THE SMART TRAVELER ENROLLMENT PROGRAM (STEP)

The Smart Traveller Enrollment Program (STEP) is a free service managed by the U.S. Department of State, Bureau of Consular Affairs and is available to U.S. citizens travelling abroad. STEP notifies the relevant U.S. embassies and consulates of a traveler's location and travel dates in a foreign country.

STEP provides the following critical services:

- Sends updated safety and security information on the related country
- Sends alerts when serious events are unfolding impacting traveler safety or security

THE SMART TRAVELER ENROLLMENT PROGRAM (STEP) (continued)

- Helps U.S. embassy personnel to locate and contact you in the event of an emergency or threatening situation

- Helps family and friends contact you in the event of an emergency

To enroll in STEP, you should visit the program website at https://step.state.gov/step/ and create a new account. Step-by-step instructions are provided on the website.

INFORMATION SECURITY

PROTECTING SENSITIVE, FOR OFFICIAL USE ONLY (FOUO), PROPRIETARY, AND PERSONAL INFORMATION ABROAD

Travelers may be targeted for information in their possession. Information theft can lead to identity theft, targeting the traveler for robbery or kidnapping or economic espionage. In addition, employees traveling abroad may find themselves in meetings with individuals whose identities or reasons for their attendance at the meeting is not clear. Travelers should be wary of responding to questions from such unidentified individuals even though they are in attendance at business meetings.

Do not leave the following unattended or unsecured in your hotel room:

- Personally identifiable information (PII) such as your picture, your home address, your home phone number
- Travel plans or trip itinerary
- Laptop computer, tablets, portable storage devices or cell phones
- Information on company's product pricing and marketing strategies
- Financial information relating to a company
- Agency employee and organizational data
- Company point to contact information
- Company or employee data

METHODS OF INFORMATION THEFT

Be aware of the following methods:

- Telephone tapping (eavesdropping)
- Fax transmission monitoring - Do not send sensitive information via fax unless using approved secure fax gateway

METHODS OF INFORMATION THEFT

- Bugging hotel rooms
- Bugging meeting rooms
- Hotel computer network monitoring
- Searching hotel room when traveler absent, to steal or photograph information
- Theft of laptop computer - Use full disk encryption to protect computer contents if lost or stolen
- Infecting laptop computer with malicious software - Update virus protection and don't open unknown files
- Flirtation or offers of sex to traveler - Be aware that this is a common method of coercion and blackmail
- Strangers attempting to elicit information in hotel bar or other social settings - Do not provide details about your role in agency or details regarding your trip
- Public eavesdropping on your discussion
- Acquiring discarded work documents from hotel room or business center trash - Do not discard sensitive information without micro-shredding first

GENERAL TIPS

Avoid places that are known as past or present terrorist targets, staging areas for holiday celebrations or protest locations.

Dress so that you blend in with locals.

Meet strangers at your work or a public location.

Do not stand in a large group of foreigners at exposed, visible public locations, e.g. bus stop, nightclub, or restaurant.

Do not discard mail or other items with your name/address on it.

Do not display/use items or objects that denote your importance, e.g. reserved parking spot or limousine.

Do not display stickers, patches, icons or tags identified with Western culture.

Do not displaying agency logo in public areas

Do not publicly observe or participate in local religious events if you are a visible minority to the local population.

DETECTING CAR TAMPERING

To check for car tampering:

- Look under car for attachments or packages
- Look in wheel wells, under bumpers, in engine compartment
- Look for signs of scraping, scratches or signs of forced entry

If you identify a suspicious object or observe indicators of tampering, MOVE AWAY from the vehicle and proceed to a safe location. Immediately contact local authorities and wait at a safe distance from your car for them to arrive. If your car was tampered with, change hotels and change your rental car.

SUSPICIOUS PACKAGE

Be alert for:

- Unusual or unknown place of origin
- No return address
- Excessive postage
- Abnormal or unusual size
- Oily stains
- Attached wires or strings
- Return address different than postmark
- Shoe polish or almond odor
- Springiness in the package walls

Steps to take:

- Leave the package, isolate the room and call security
- DO NOT examine the package

ATMOSPHERICS AND THREAT INDICATORS

Be alert for individuals making eye contact with you.

If you notice a change in local routines or patterns on the street, be aware – this may indicate danger.

If you notice a change in local conditions, e.g. children taken inside, shops closing down or unusual lack of traffic – this may indicate danger.

Repetitive behavior like a repeated drive-by may be surveillance on an area targeted for terrorism.

TRAVEL BOOKING AND AIRCRAFT SEATING

Choose a window seat in the middle section of the aircraft. Window seats are less accessible to hijackers and the middle of the plane offers alternative escape routes.

Request an emergency aisle window seat. These seats offer the best opportunity for aircraft escape. If one is not available, try to book a seat one or two rows from the emergency exit.

If window seats are not available in the middle section, book a seat in the rear of the plane. This is away from the center of aggression, which is usually near the cockpit in the event of a hijacking.

Try to book with a US flag carrier.

Adhere to your agency's guidance for making travel arrangements.

DRESS FOR ANONYMITY

Do not wear distinct military, government or other uniforms.

Do not wear military, government or first responder casual wear, e.g. FBI baseball cap, US Army or NYPD T-shirt, etc.

Keep official military or government identification separate from wallet and personal identification.

If you have official identification with you, look for a place on the aircraft to quickly and discreetly dispose of it if necessary.

If you have an arm tattoo that depicts an association with the military or other national institutions, wear long sleeves to cover it.

REPORTING SUSPICIOUS BEHAVIOR

If you spot suspicious behavior on the aircraft:

- Write down the seat number of the suspicious individual
- Include a brief description of the individual
- Briefly describe the suspicious behavior
- Casually provide the note to a flight attendant

Always keep a pen and a cell phone in your possession and accessible from your aircraft seat.

IN THE RARE EVENT OF AN AIR ACCIDENT

Some facts:

- 10% of fatalities are caused by the crash impact
- 90% of fatalities are caused by smoke and fire
- 80% of all accidents occur on takeoff and landing

The top bins will open in an accident or severe turbulence. Be prepared to protect yourself from heavy projectiles.

When seated, take note of your location in the aircraft. Knowledge of surroundings is critical to escape. Know your escape route before it's needed.

If you are removing the emergency door, sit down to do it. The person behind you may be pushing, making it impossible to remove while standing.

Never go back into a burning aircraft.

TAXIS

Vary use of approved taxi companies.

Do not let someone you don't know direct you to a particular taxi.

Do not get into a taxi if the driver has a companion.

Taxi licensing:

- Check to ensure the taxi is licensed
- If the license is not displayed, ask to see it before getting in
- Check that the driver's face matches the face on the license

Make sure there is adequate fuel in the car for your trip.

Specify the route you want the driver to take on a map.

Make sure the driver follows the route you provided.

PUBLIC BUSES, SUBWAYS AND TRAINS

Vary modes of commercial transit.

Do not use desolate or sparsely populated bus/subway stops.

Vary choice of departure and arrival stations.

Avoid mass transit at night – take a taxi or private transportation service as an alternative.

If traveling on an overnight train, be vigilant – theft is common.

Do not accept food or drink from strangers – it may be drugged.

Notify the conductor if you spot anything suspicious – police are often assigned to trains and subways.

CAR RENTALS

Ask for a recent model, medium sized sedan.

Make sure there are no decals identifying the vehicle as a rental.

Unless absolutely necessary, do not rent an oversized SUV or luxury model vehicle.

Do not try to save money with a cheaper, older model vehicle from a discount company.

Familiarize yourself with the vehicle before leaving:

- Inspect for scratches, scrapes, or other marks that can be mistaken later for signs of forced entry or tampering
- Inspect tires for good tread

DRIVING FUNDAMENTALS

Always maintain at least 50% filled fuel tank.

Always lock doors and keep windows to drive/park the vehicle.

Avoid overnight parking on streets.

Try to avoid parking lots where keys are left with attendant – if unavoidable, provide ignition key only.

Back into a parking spot so you can drive out quickly if needed.

If you need directions to your hotel, call the hotel:

- Use a cell phone or public phone vs. asking a stranger
- Ask for directions that use major highways
- Do not provide your exact location
- Do not ask the clerk at the airport rental car desk
- Do not use the airport's hotel courtesy phone

GENERAL TIPS

When checking into your room:

- Identify the location of the fire exits on your floor
- Check operational status of door/window locks
- Test the room telephone to ensure it is operational and understand how to make emergency calls with it

Do not accept visits or deliveries to your room from strangers.

Do not answer the phone with your name.

When you leave the room:

- Leave the TV on – with sound
- Leave the lights on
- Put the Do Not Disturb sign on your door

Check for evidence of tampering or forced entry upon returning to your room.

Remove personal identification items before leaving room, e.g. business cards, prescription drugs or credit card receipts.

Do not leave sensitive agency information or devices containing such information (laptop, cell phone, memory sticks, etc.) unsecured or alone in room.

ROOM SELECTION

Ask for a room between the 4th and 8th floors. This is the safe zone to survive a street level explosion and make a rapid exit from the building.

Ask for a room that opens into the interior of the hotel, or one that does not face a major street.

IF YOU SUSPECT YOU ARE BEING FOLLOWED TO YOUR ROOM

Stop in a public area of the hotel for a few minutes.

If the individual(s) continue to act suspiciously, report them to hotel security.

If you spot the individual(s) following you on your floor:

- Take the nearest fire exit down to the lobby, move quickly but don't panic
- Report the individual(s) to hotel security
- Ask for an escort back to your room
- CONSIDER CHANGING HOTELS

IF A STRANGER INITIATES CONVERSATION

Hotels are social environments. It is not unusual for a stranger to strike up casual conversation. If this happens:

- Engage in light conversation
- Do not offer your name
- Do not provide your nationality – if the stranger is persistent, use an excuse to terminate the conversation
- Do not provide the reason for your trip or nature of your business
- Do not say how long you are staying or if traveling alone
- Do not indicate which floor/room you are staying in
- Do not reveal if you are traveling alone

RANDOMIZING DAILY ROUTINES

GENERAL TIPS

Do not establish identifiable patterns in the way you carry out your daily routine.

If you leave the hotel during the workday, vary your routes from and back to the hotel.

Vary your use of hotel services, e.g. pool or fitness center.

Mail packages at different times of day and from various mailing locations.

If you are staying in a high threat location for a long duration, change hotels every 2 weeks.

Do not set business meetings for the same time – vary the times that you meet.

Do not shop from the same stores or plazas – use alternate shopping locations.

ENTERTAINMENT AND SOCIAL OUTINGS

Vary the times that you depart to your social destination.

Do not become a regular visitor to any particular establishments.

Be vigilant and protect your drinks/food from drugging.

Be aware of elicitation attempts (conversational attempts to gain sensitive personal or professional information) by seemingly friendly strangers striking up a conversation.

RANDOMIZE HOW YOU DRESS

Randomize your outfits: try to show variation in your outfits by wearing different colors and styles for your shirts, hats, ties, dresses, etc.

RANDOMIZE YOUR MOVEMENTS

Chart at least three different routes to frequently visited destinations.

Take different routes – do not become predictable in your choice of routes.

Alter your time of departure each day.

If using mass transit, vary your departure and return bus stops, subway stops or train stations.

RANDOMIZE YOUR DINING

Alter your dining times each day.

Vary the time between your breakfast and departure from the hotel.

Do not eat lunch/dinner with the same local person every day – even if they are a trusted work associate.

Vary your dining habits – it is safer to dine within the hotel, but do not always use the same restaurant if possible.

Randomly choose between the hotel restaurants and room service.

WHAT NOT TO RANDOMIZE

Contact family members on a regular and predetermined schedule.

Check in with your office regularly and let them know when to expect your next call.

Always maintain measures designed to protect you, e.g. leave lights and TV on and put 'Do Not Disturb' sign on door when leaving hotel room.

SURVEILLANCE

INDICATORS THAT YOU ARE UNDER SURVEILLANCE

Take note of suspicious or repeated actions which may indicate that you are under hostile surveillance:

- A car driving past you at a low rate of speed
- Different vehicles occupied by the same people
- Cars flashing headlights to each other
- A vehicle driving back and forth along the same roadway
- A vehicle parked in an unusual spot
- Individual(s) staring at you from afar
- Individual(s) quickly look away when you look towards them
- Individual(s) who seem to be following you
- Individual(s) engaged in seemingly normal behavior but they keep reappearing as you move
- An individual taking your photograph or appearing to take notes on your appearance or activities

Scan people and vehicles within your vicinity.

Familiarize yourself with the local environment so abnormalities will be apparent to you.

Scrutinize utility workers, street vendors, people waiting for a bus, or vehicle drive-by's.

Look for familiar faces and vehicles that you may have seen before.

Remain vigilant and alert.

PATTERN VIOLATION INDICATORS

Pattern violation is a good indicator that there are surveillance operations underway. Look for signs that normal patterns are being violated:

PATTERN VIOLATION INDICATORS (continued)

Pattern violation is a good indicator that there are surveillance operations underway. Look for signs that normal patterns are being violated:

- Vendors in area without customers
- Utility workers without proper equipment
- Utility workers standing around not working
- People at bus stands who don't depart on buses
- Repeated drive-by's

SOCIAL ENGINEERING

Social engineering is a method of deception where an adversary used a false pretext or fake identity to gain access to a secure area or protected information. Social Engineering can also be used to conduct surveillance within controlled or public areas.

Be alert and aware of:

- Visitors to the workplace, e.g. a technician, delivery person, job applicant, etc.
- Utility workers on your hotel guest floor
- Telephone callers asking hotel staff to provide information about you e.g. a call from a courier asking what time you will be in the hotel

GENERAL TIPS

If you suspect that you are under surveillance, DO NOT PANIC.

Do not openly confront suspected individual(s).

Do not indicate that you know you are under surveillance.

Notify your agency and the hotel security contact.

Remember to do the things that will make you a hard target and cross you off their list of potential targets:

- Move to a public location
- Randomize your movements
- If you have a rental car:
    - See if you can return the car and get a replacement
    - Take a companion with you to return the car
    - Rent a new car from a different rental company
- If you are under surveillance in your hotel (or followed back to your hotel):
    - Remain in a public area
    - Notify hotel security
    - Get an escort to your room
    - Check out and stay in a different hotel

METHODS ON FOOT

If you think you are being followed on foot:

- Change your pace or pause to window shop – observe the suspect in the window reflection
- Note if the suspect pauses or adjusts their pace to match yours

METHODS ON FOOT (continued)

If you think you are being followed on foot:

- Change your pace or pause to window shop – observe the suspect in the window reflection
- Note if the suspect has adjusted to your pace or paused when you did
- Retrace your steps and look for familiar faces to see if you are being watched
- Move directly to a secure, public location, report the incident to local authorities
- CONSIDER CHANGING HOTELS

METHODS WHILE DRIVING

If you suspect you are under surveillance while driving, make turns and check for continued surveillance or use turning indicator
but go straight, checking if the suspect has done the same. If confirmed, drive to the front of a hotel or a public location at a normal speed and seek security or police.

Defensive driving techniques:

- Do not drive in the inner lanes – drive in the outside (curb) lane
- Maintain eight feet between the car in front of you (not much more or less) when you come to a stop
- Avoid chokepoints or getting boxed in
- Do not slow down to let the pursuing vehicle pass
- Do not leave a main road

If you are in a rental car, return the car and rent a new car from a different rental company.

ATTACK INDICATORS & COUNTERMEASURES

EMERGING THREATS AND DECISIVE ACTIONS

While driving in remote or unsafe areas:

1. **A cyclist falls in front of your car:**

   Try to avoid the cyclist but DO NOT STOP – keep driving

2. **A flagman or workman suspiciously stops your car:**

   Turn the car around immediately and take an alternate route back – do not speak or motion to flagman/workman

3. **A disabled vehicle or accident victims lying on the road:**

   DO NOT STOP – continue driving – if the road is blocked turn the car around immediately and take an alternate route back

4. **Another vehicle strikes your vehicle from behind:**

   Do not get out. If you come under attack – SOUND HORN AND CONTINUE DRIVING – if necessary, ram the car to escape – if required, drive over curb or median at a 30° to 45° angle at a maximum speed of 35 MPH / 56 KPH

5. **A suspicious motorcyclist drives between lanes to approach your vehicle:**

   Move your car to block the motorcycle and then escape by driving over median or curb if necessary

When reserving a car for transportation from the airport, your hotel or other locations:

- Always reserve from a well-known and trusted business (you can ask your hotel for recommendations)

- Ask the driver for company identification when they arrive

- If approached by driver who asks your name and claims it is on their list, ask to see your name before proceeding

EMERGING THREATS AND DECISIVE ACTIONS (continued)

While walking:

Individual(s) attempt to abduct you in a vehicle:

- Yell at abductor(s) to stop
- Yell for bystanders to call police
- Yell at bystanders that you are being abducted and need help
- Place people, other vehicles or objects between you and the abductor(s)
- If you can't escape, fight back by any means

If you are caught in the middle of a terrorist attack:

- Dive for cover – do not run
- If you must move, belly crawl or roll

If you see or suspect the imminent use of an explosive device:

- Lay flat on the ground, with your stomach against the ground
- Press your feet and knees tightly together with the soles of your feet facing toward the source of explosion
- Place your hands over your ears and keep your arms close to your body – this will protect vital arteries in your neck and your rib cage
- The blast will rise in a cone shape from the source of the blast, so the closer you are to the ground, the less you are exposed to the explosion
- DO NOT HOLD YOUR BREATH - take short breaths to avoid lung collapse and internal bleeding from the shock wave, which follows immediately after the explosion
- If you are unharmed after the incident, immediately move away from the source of the explosion and seek shelter in a safe location

EXPOSURE TO ESPIONAGE WHILE ABROAD

Some foreign governments engage in espionage and intelligence collection against visitors or assist espionage by their domestic companies. U.S. citizens may be exposed to a range of tactics from rudimentary to highly sophisticated.

WHAT ARE THE INFORMATION TARGETS?

- Travel plans and itinerary information for agency personnel
- Computer and network passwords and login information
- Formulas, processes, procedures or other engineering data

HOSTILE TACTICS

- Telephone tapping (eavesdropping)
- Cell phone and fax scanning and monitoring
- Hotel computer network monitoring
- Bugging hotel rooms and meeting rooms
- Searching and theft from hotel rooms while traveler is out
- Flirtation, offers of sex in order to elicit company information
- Plying travelers with drinks or drugs

REPORTING SECURITY INCIDENTS

REPORTING SECURITY INCIDENTS

If you have been involved in a security incident and you are traveling for business, you should report the incident to your company and inform your embassy. Take countermeasures described earlier to reduce your exposure to the threat.

If you are traveling for pleasure, inform your embassy and take countermeasures described earlier to reduce your exposure to the threat.

If you have been the victim of a crime, make a report with local police and report the incident to your embassy. Inform your company if you are traveling for business.

IN THE EVENT OF A NATURAL DISASTER

If your location is under threat of a natural disaster, contact your embassy for updates on the situation and to make sure they are aware of your location. Contact your company as well, if you are on a business trip and coordinate next steps, then update your family on your situation.

If your location suffers a natural disaster and you require evacuation, attempt to contact your embassy, and then your company. If you cannot contact the embassy, travel there directly. You will be given instructions regarding evacuation, if required. Stay in contact with your company and update your family on your situation.